TERMINAL SURREAL

POEMS

TERMINAL SURREAL

MARTHA SILANO

ACRE
CINCINNATI 2025

Acre Books is made possible by the support of the Robert and Adele Schiff Foundation and the Department of English at the University of Cincinnati.

Copyright © 2025 by Martha Silano
All rights reserved
Printed in the United States of America

ISBN-13 (pbk) 978-1-946724-94-6
ISBN-13 (ebook) 978-1-946724-95-3

Designed by Barbara Neely Bourgoyne
Cover art: iStock/Oleksii Kriachko

No part of this work may be reproduced or transmitted in any form or by any means, electronic or mechanical, including photocopying and recording, or by any information storage or retrieval system, without express written permission, except in the case of brief quotations embodied in critical articles and reviews.

The press is based at the University of Cincinnati, Department of English, Arts & Sciences Hall, Room 248, PO Box 210069, Cincinnati, OH, 45221-0069.

Acre Books titles may be purchased at a discount for educational use. For information please email business@acre-books.com.

CONTENTS

I
Can't Complain, ... 3
Flying Rats 5
Self-Appraisal at 62 7
I'm Not So Good at Corpse Pose 8
Mistakes Were Made 10
What's Terrible 11
Possible Diagnosis 12
It's Benzene, It's Ash, It's Lead, ... 13
Unambiguously, ... 14
Abecedarian by the Crazy Lady with ALS 15
Elegy with Exhaust Fan and Robin Song at Dusk 16
I Have Thoughts Fed by the Sun, ... 17
Mortal 18
On a Bench Facing West 19
Death Poem 20

II
Orders of Operation 23
Since You're Alive 24
When I Learn *Catastrophically* 25
To-Do List 27

Abecedarian with ALS 28
I am the last loss, ... 29
When I'm on the Bed 30
At the Mycological Society Survivors Banquet 31
I didn't understand Keats's "Ode to a Nightingale" 33
Is This My Last Ferry Trip? 35
Terminal Surreal 36
Abecedarian on a Friday Morning 37
Self-Elegies 38

III

When I Can't Get Out of Bed 43
What You See Isn't What You Get 44
It's Difficult to Understand 45
Today 46
Wake-Up Call 47
Why I Want to Be a Noble Gas 48
Sometimes It's Nice to Be Taken Away 49
Spas of the Mind 51
The Busy Roadways of the Dead 52
Cars & Such 53
Leo 54
When My Phone Tells Me 55
Why I'd Make a Great Chemist 56

IV

John Muir Elementary 59
Next Week We Have a Doudle Assinment 61
There Are Thousands of Pleasures, ... 63
Double Triptych for the Months of Nectarine and Plum 65
Key Grove 67
How It Is Today 69

What I Didn't Realize 70
How to Fall 71
After Dropping My Son Off at College, ... 73
Poem on My Son's Twenty-Third Birthday 74
My Nineteen-Year-Old Daughter Is My Personal Assistant, ... 76
A Poem about Twinflower 77
Spoon Theory 78
Smile 79
If We Didn't Leave the Task to Backhoes 80
Legacy 81

V

I Found Small Slices of Joy 85
I Always Wake Up Happy 86
Taking a Walk with Rimbaud 88
Postcard from Some Unknown Part of My Brain 89
What I'll Miss 90
I Want to Be an Adirondack Chair 92
She's Pretty Much Who She Was, ... 94
You-n-Me 95
Poetry, ... 96
Portrait of Apple Cinnamon Mush, Chobani Yogurt Drink, and BiPAP 98
Before and After: A Quasi-Abecedarian 99
Making the Best of It 100
You Are Much More Than This Body 101

ACKNOWLEDGMENTS 103

I

CAN'T COMPLAIN,

I mean, at least it's not 106 degrees. At least I'm not hearing
a loud popping sound in my knee, followed by swelling.
I had no idea those pops are referred to

as *pathological noise*. What a great name for a band.
But seriously, I'm good. Hoping for the same
with you—no aphids in your begonias,
no sore senses or Columns

of Creation pain. I hope your cupboards shine like Orion.
That humor hangs in your closet with the raincoats,
that you haven't been ejected

from the room of ineffable calm, that your days are more freesia,
less filth. I heard on the radio yesterday we need to cut
emissions by 45%, like, now, but it turns out

most countries are having trouble cutting them by 3%. *Who-ee*,
it sounds like 2030's gonna be soggy. We'll all be sporting
flame-retardant flight dresses for the wildfires I doubt

will be canceled. What shoes pair well with my drenched-pot-roast
shift? I was thinking a strappy mountain-high sole
with an electrically spinning heel.

Also, a vibrating instep. At the not-prom, we'll swap our favorite
pre-mass-extinction tales, awake until the stars extinguish
like wicks. But enough about me: what will you be

for Halloween? I was thinking I'd be a belly-dancing zombie queen,
stand at the door with a bowl of Skittles, evoking terror
in the beatifically brave come-knockers. Here,
let me pin that corsage. I always loved

orchids—too bad yours got scorched on its little foray to a planet
some idiots think we can live on. O, space! O, to fall
into the arms of a gap of blue. Not that I'm blue,

but really, I hope you're well, that your *wheeee* hasn't cracked,
that your bones aren't talking. I hope every other minute
is a sparkler that never burns out.

FLYING RATS

with apologies to Mary Oliver

Actually? You do have to be good.
For real? You kinda do have to walk,
if not literally on your knees,
then figuratively on your knees,
or if not on your "knees," then
in really cruddy, falling-apart
grandma tennies with worn-out
orthotics she bought back in the '90s
at Kmart. For, like, a hundred miles—
from downtown Los Angeles
to the Bakersfield McDonald's.
Also, guess what? You do have to say
I'm sorry many times a day for things
like forgetting to tighten the faucet,
or leaving the gas on, or hitting
your kids, even if only once
on the bottom. Not gonna lie:
you can't go around all jellyfish,
all shell-less mollusk, scrolling
Instagram or watching *Love Island*.
We can talk to each other about
what pains us (me: not going to visit
my deathbed mother; you: having
to gain weight), but let's be honest:
saying "Meanwhile the world goes on"
doesn't cut it. Why? Because yeah,
there's sun and pebbles, prairies
and trees, mountains and rivers,
but let's not airbrush out the number
of acres of US forest lost to wildfires
this past summer: seven and a half

million. Meanwhile the geese
are shitting all over the playground grass,
the walkways and cement barriers.
Not high up, but dragging their butts
across mowed-down blackberry brambles.
Okay, so you're lonely, and the world
offers you *Itself*? Calls to you like
one of these cobra chickens? Yeah,
yeah, pretty harsh. Pretty f-ing harsh.

SELF-APPRAISAL AT 62

Sometimes, it's okay to compare yourself to a cracked terracotta pot,
ask *What about this place called Earth?* though it's okay
to not ask permission to appear

in a low-cut gold lamé dress higher up the thigh than someone, somewhere,
considers appropriate. Mainly, it's staying in your reclined movie seat
till the very last credit, till you find out who wrote every song,

including "What Was I Made For?" Such a good question! Ask yourself,
and I will too. But mostly? Adventures in vexing. Dostoevsky-ishly
nuanced. Feeling more at home in my bosom-buddy body,

yet wrapped in every glass of pinot grigio, every oops-no-SPF suntanning afternoon.
Something like *inexorably*, not to be discouraging. As I often say to my life partner,
would you rather the alternative? Despite juicy maggots and blowflies,

I carry on with the bubbly, my plate piled high with pasta alla norma,
always stop at that bakery in Cashmere with the baguette straight out
of Anjou. It's too soon to know how bad it will get,

but for now there are sexual pleasure tools out the wazoo. I mean,
the MRI revealed a white spot on my right frontal lobe,
so I Dr. Googled: *possible early sign of dementia*.

SO fun! (as I like to text), but today all my Nutter Butters and Lorna Doones
are exactly where they belong, and I'm coming and going
like a subway line to Queens.

It's not quite a choose your own adventure, though I do make sure
to roll down grassy hills, to stand in line for an ice cream novelty
when the rainbow van pulls up, to make a little lotus blossom

with my fingertips. Maybe it's a good idea to take a long, good look
in the mirror, ask *Change? Why would I change?* To give
the future both the finger and a thumbs-up.

I'M NOT SO GOOD AT CORPSE POSE

Sitting in lotus position, the yoga teacher reminds us to thank our bodies
for what they've just done, half-moon and reverse warrior,
side angle and downward-facing dog.

We've just woken from the dead, having been in deep rest
when she roused us with a clanging bell
that sounds Doppler-ish

thanks to unstable Wi-Fi. Śavāsana. I always try to focus on the rain
slapping my studio windows, on a plane about to land at Sea–Tac,
but I pretty much always can't

because I'm thinking about the garbage, how I have to collect it
from each little wicker basket, sort it (don't want
my orange peels ending up in a landfill,

or the toilet paper rolls anywhere but the recycling bin).
The bell is tolling, and I'm supposed
to be reviving myself,

but instead I've been lugging the bins to the curb, checking
on the spinach starts, kicking gravel out of the driveway,
back to its home in the cracks along the side porch.

What can I say? I make a pretty bad cadaver? That it will take
turning me into ash or compost to get me to stop
obsessing about the next thing on my list?

It's 7 a.m., and already I've clocked 45 *move* minutes on my Apple Watch.
Hurray for me! Now I will find peace beside the space heater
with a cup of turmeric and ginger tea

supposed to help my aching knees. No, I haven't graduated to bodhisattva
quite yet. The door's ajar, and the cats rush in like the air
through the gap in a door

I'll maybe, at the end, float through, past the oldest cedars
in Seattle, toward the dead who live inside each eagle
invisibly squealing.

MISTAKES WERE MADE

The weather app said the wind was from the south and west.
It was from the north and east.

The sinus doctor said it's your brain. Maybe you had a stroke in your sleep.
It was a benign nodule in one of my lymph nodes.

The pan said nonstick.
The fried egg stuck.

Another doctor ordered a swallow test. I chewed a cracker
mixed with barium, learned my right vocal cord was weak.

I went out on a boat. A muscle spasm in my torso roiled
like the surf. When I googled my symptoms,

I found ALS. When a friend said *Stop it, you can't
diagnose yourself*, I figured she was right.

All the testing. All the tests. The doctor who said
If I were in Vegas, I'd bet it was all due

to stress. The last stop was the eighth floor,
Neurology. They looked at my tongue,

asked me to spit in a tube to be sent off to a lab
where they'd check to see if it was inherited.

The weather report said *sun, sun, sun*.
It rained.

WHAT'S TERRIBLE

after Dorianne Laux

When the alpenglow fades and the ridicule flares. When the morass appears, three-quarters pestilence, one-quarter shale. A whining moth that morphs to a motif. A manager defending a pervert. A mandate to spray Roundup. A flea soiree. Flawed soil. When the moor is too briquette to sleep. When the stripes are too broad to see the rorqual for the *Cyamus*. A broken fin. Downturn far enough to throb. Jettison when it loses its riffle. Nonsense you can't plait. A ridiculing jester, harder to listen to than traitors, than sitars at a Lunatic Éclair Siege. When the ATM eats your cardigan, your caress. You forgot to charge your phone. The plantains didn't align. You need chemo, but CVS is flush out of toxins. Wastelands. Horsewhips. No map, no toilet paper, no headlamp. The sound of windbags through pineapple groves. The scent of Vieux-Boulogne. The menacing shadows of hemlocks.

POSSIBLE DIAGNOSIS

What's that stone, that one stone edging
toward the edge? In Italian, for spider,
say *ragno*. Say *web*

in a musical spell. I was with a friend,
on my last round. When I told her
I might be dying,

she was my dictator of snow, holding me
and my gone-berserk nerves.
I told her my mother

puts the relevant clues in crossword puzzles:
Riley, *refs*, and *palomas*. Isn't she
the best cheerer-upper ever?

Maybe I'm a witch for the drama cauldron,
maybe I just need more sleep, more
nooky, cookies-n-cream.

Old and unheavy, in need of rest. God?
I don't quite believe, but at night
I let myself go fetal,

hands pressed like that plastic pair Svennie found
at a thrift store in Shelton. To breathe.
To swallow. Now I understand:

incurable might not be the worst thing. Upsides, like creasing
the cloth napkins, carrying them down to their home
in a living room drawer,

admiring the spotted towhee making a ruckus in dead leaves.
I thought it would be like a thumb coming down
on a spider's body, but it was not.

IT'S BENZENE, IT'S ASH, IT'S LEAD,

and many other things dissipating.
So sorry, but despite this, elephants
prop up their feet, listen for their herd.

Wasn't there always awe, punctuated
with grief? WonderPain. MarvelWoe.
WowLoss. Weren't we always elegies

with spleens? But today all I care about
is the Island Marble Butterfly making
a comeback. Coming back in all its green-

and-white-mottled glory. The average dreamer
dreams four to seven times a night. Whether or not
we believe in karma, Carhartt, or chocolate-

covered ice cream squares called Klondikes,
our shoulders, trapezius muscles, and lungs
all look pretty much the same when cut open.

Passing torched trees, garbage gyres,
the smokestacks of Longview and Tacoma,
we might not react exactly the same,

but we all feel something, right? Hair
and trembling. And when a diaphragm
sharply contracts, any one of us will hiccup.

UNAMBIGUOUSLY,

I wasn't manifesting my best rain, my best evening gown
of cool. In my vegetable age, I shriveled like a thirsty
gourd. Untranslatably heated, I could not

be dazzled. Emeralds were no longer my philosophy.
What the f happened to me and my life-giving
monsoons? I no longer have the lips

of a boat orchid. The mango juice of me has been squeezed out.
Had I, as my mother would ask, overdone it? Well, yeah,
sorta. The rum drained out of my every mai tai,

the gin and Campari from every negroni. My oeuvre slammed shut
like the freezer in the McDonald's basement on Route 27,
the one holding the frozen pre-chopped onions.

Befallen and befalling. *Sea* and *say* submerged. Some island named Danger:
Rising. It was all thirsty horizons. Striated, tasteless guavas. No one
named Lily or Alamanda, only the ragged tragedy

of a worn-out body. Sultry and palm-less. Oh, the unmanageable
hibiscus-ness of it! Delight gone dead like a scorching night
in Tangier. Beware,

for it can steal your hound. Render you essence-less, dumb
like a clump of earth. For it torches tendrilled skies,
scorches your brightest bananas.

ABECEDARIAN BY THE CRAZY LADY WITH ALS

ALS clinic begins now! We start by checking lungs.
BTW, it says here you had a bipolar episode, a
comorbidity, cuz when you had your son
decades ago, we saw it in your chart, you became
erratic! Went nuts! We don't mean to be rude, but
(fucking) seriously, you know what? That
gyrating noggin of yours that makes it impossibly
hard to close your eyes? THAT'S NOT ALS.
It's time for an eye appointment, you wacky hatter
just making shit up. It's all in your head. Those
knocking-rocking eye-opening fasciculations?
Lunatic-speak! It's either depression or
mania, but likely it's brain inflammation, though
nope—we did that test and shucks. So, what this
old owl told me is he's never heard of it, and this
pigeon said it's really cuz you're pyscho, unstable,
quacky, gonzo, nutsy, wacko, out of your cedar,
round the jay, up the pole, crackers, batty, loony,
Saint Christina mad, barmy, batty, bananas for Cocoa Puffs,
too screwy to unscrew a red-chested cuckoo's neck,
unhinged. What I recommend is doubling your
Wellbutrin, or whatever it is you're on, quadrupling the
Xanax, and let's check back in three months. 'Til then,
you're a nonsensical, preposterous, confounding,
zebralike fruitcake. A true *Lisa, Bright and Dark*.

ELEGY WITH EXHAUST FAN AND ROBIN SONG AT DUSK

Now that *The War to End All Wars* is a slug in the compost bin of history,
I'm never going to say a batch of fudge brownies is done, even when
the knife stuck into the middle comes out clean.

After I've vanished, I'll get a new hairdo—a pageboy or a bob.
After I've swum past August's dry moss, after my eyebrows
cascade past my collarbones, I'll rename myself

Apostrophe, possessor of bends in the trail. Wear my cutoffs
like a pair of bricks, sink into the intimate ground.
When I disappear, I'll no longer collaborate

with the house finches but hitch my trailer to a gust. It turns out all this time
I'd been hiding in a patch of penstemon, which meant the moon to me.
I could lift my head, listen to the ruckus of hummingbirds,

never imagining I'd be banished from London and Paris,
all the towns in between. It was like a flame
in a campfire igniting from an ember,

tumbling in the wind, a flame that set an entire valley
on fire. A flame I know
I can't put out.

I HAVE THOUGHTS FED BY THE SUN,

and I have thoughts fed by fear.
The sun-thoughts leave me clumsy,

giddy. Tumbling into persuadable lakes.
The fear-thoughts are like the squirrels

claiming my neighbor's chimney,
make of my brain a panic closet.

My sun-thoughts beam me back
to the iridescence of starlings,

while fear knits a dark petticoat
of macabre, a dance so not like

an Oregon swallowtail. Wild
carrot it's not, nor the sage

of the high desert plains.
Here: take this dark one,

replace it with a daisy,
with the sun beating down

on the two cherry trees in my yard,
the fruit so difficult to reach.

MORTAL

at the sink,
spraying leftover meat sauce
down the drain. Near the toaster,

snuffing out sugar ants
with a turquoise rag. Mortal
as a door slowly opening, the cat

you rescued in 2009, just shy
of your daughter's fourth birthday,
when you taught her to make strawberry shortcake.

Mortal while you rest, reveling
in your 119% lungs. Mortal as you wipe
handprints from the fridge, remind yourself

anger has mostly been your MO.
Mortal Earth. Mortal sun. Mortal mother
and how, you wonder, would she react to your dying

so much younger than Frank Sinatra crooned,
living to a hundred and five, like your ratty hoody collection,
your dented Elantra parked outside your mortal house on a cold

February morning—newly serviced, ready to take you,
as if immortal, to San Juan Island. Mortal as sleet, as snow,
as a breast anticipating touch. Mortal like a cold or warm mother,

a stone, a seam, a fearsome river
with hundreds of violet-green swallows,
the sound of a garbage can dragged to the curb.

ON A BENCH FACING WEST

at 4:05 p.m. The wind is up.
A raft of common mergansers.
A bunch of herons on the floating dock.
Some crows there too.
It's hard not to think
of all the times I jogged past this.
Ten-minute mile.
It's hard to not make up a story
that everyone I pass on this trail is healthy.

Today my day spent figuring out how to climb stairs
less, how to conserve my energy for things like this
half-mile/half-hour walk. Forcing myself to slow
to a 29.37-minute-mile pace.

A woman said she counted thirteen herons.
The luck of it!!
And now the gratitude list:
Only one foot cramp.
My son did his laundry without me having to ask.
My daughter, insisting I read *The Waves*,
sent me images of underlined words
about being a stalk: *My roots go down
to the depths of the world.*

A pair of mallards. A pair of . . .
what are they called? They have chevrons
on their breasts. Oh yeah: gadwalls!
Wind blowing harder. Something about being
all fiber. I envy the joggers. The joggers,
and those who die in their sleep.

DEATH POEM

Death is the one-day-alive mayfly clinging to a watering can.
When the grass turns brown, how can I not think of death?
In my heart, death lives like a mama raccoon with her two young.
We haven't figured out a way to undo death.
Death awaits the pigeon on a roof, says the Cooper's hawk.
It's not cool to mention corpse beetles when there's a death.
Did you know there's a death's-head hawkmoth?
A scrub jay squawks *death, death, death!*
Dragonflies and death: they live about six months.
Eating is for sure some kind of elaborate death feast.
Sometimes death is invisible, especially when we laugh.
Our planet: one big tribute concert to death.
Death be not proud, says John Donne, but death is proud, I think.
Everything ends up being an ode to death.

II

ORDERS OF OPERATION

First thing, my hair began to weep. Wept like sea oats, the roots of which
are forty feet deep. First thing, my torso quivered like mud
in a 192-mile-an-hour wind. Like a seed head

in a Category 6, its vibrating underground rhizomes. One night,
in my bathroom mirror, I thought I saw my heartbeat
in my bicep. What was that quote

about a bitter heart? *In the desert I saw a creature, naked, bestial . . .*
A naked, bestial creature eating his bitter heart. What a wild image,
right? Liking the bitter taste *Because it is bitter,* the way an osprey

must love the taste of salt on its mouth as it dives for a fish,
succeeds. It must know that feeling of victory, of settling
into a palmetto, or perching at the top of a building

to feast. After a while, I listened with my eyebrows. After a while,
I listened to the sunlight in my pectorals and glutes,
the non-noise of sleep, which made me anxious.

And ahhh, what was this thing with my voice, why was it getting harder
to swallow and speak? When I googled, I found hideous things.
To lightly fly away, like a rosy maple moth. Slowly,

but not too slow. To flutter in the key of yellow and pink,
without coughing or wheezing,
without a batlike resistance.

To go without weeping or creaking, without too much hoopla,
like these little precious creamy-white wings,
like these rosy-pink markings

on the margins and bases, which do a kind of breezy,
like oat grass, which does a little able flying,
then slows down so lightly, so lovely.

SINCE YOU'RE ALIVE

you bother less with things like pants,
stroll into the kitchen at 5 a.m.
wearing the $5 briefs you found in a pile

of $5 briefs at Target, floppy pink flowers
against a green background, note just how bony
your bony ass, as this thing called *denervation*

begins its dance in your biceps and shoulders,
though isn't it more like August in the vineyards
of the Willamette Valley? Crushing time.

Nothing's bleeding, no ghosts signaling
you're gonna be fine, but when you call your brother,
tell him you want some of who you were

in the family plot, a light goes on
in your beat-up Elantra:
What's that goddamn light doing on?

Though the sky's unlit by 4 p.m., unlit for over fifteen hours,
which was always rough, but now, my God.
At home, you focus on the fireplace

while fearing the same flutter beneath your right eye,
which your love insists is barely visible,
but for how long? And what had I

wished for? Had it been Venice,
the Uffizi, one more hike to Mason Lake,
Spiraea douglasii along its shore?

All of it, of course, all of it in unison,
that scent of early decay, that first
turn from summer to fall.

WHEN I LEARN *CATASTROPHICALLY*

is an anagram of *amyotrophic lateral sclerosis*.
When I learn I probably have a couple years,
maybe (catastrophically) less, crossword puzzles
begin to feel meaningless, though not the pair
of buffleheads, not the red cardinal of my heart.
The sky does all sorts of marvelously uncatastrophic
things that winter I shimmy between science
& song, between widgeons & windows, weather
& its invitation to walk. Walking, which becomes
my *lose less*, my *less morsels*, my *lose smile*
while *more sore looms*. Sometimes I wander
for hours, my mile pace over half an hour,
everyone passing the lady at dusk talking
to herself about *looming rooms, soil lies, ire
& else*. Chuckling about my mileage gone down
the toilet, I plant the *rose* of before, the *oil* of after.
As each breath elevates to miracle, I become
both more & less of who I'd been, increasingly
less concerned about the dishes in the sink,
more worried about the words in my notebooks,
all those unfinished poems. I remember the fear
of getting lost if I left the main trail. I remember
molehills, actual molehills, piles of salty roe,
mountains of limes. Catastrophically, it's rare:
one in 500,000, but then I learned the odds
of being born: one in 42 billion, though not sure
how they calculate, or the chances of the cosmos
having just the right amount of force to not
break apart. *Less smiles. More lose. Miser miles.*
A sis & bro whom I'll leave like a sinking island,
Ferdinandea, that submerged volcano in Sicily,
though let's be real: I was more *pen mole* than *lava*,
more a looming annoyance than a bridge

to some continent. I'd wanted to be composted,
but it would cost $9K to convert me to dirt, so I opted
for whatever was easiest to carry across state lines,
some of me beside my mother & father, bits of me
on San Juan Island, at Jakle's Lagoon & Seward Park,
where I'd wandered like a *morose remorse*,
a *lore-less reel*, a *miser silo*, a doddering crow.

TO-DO LIST

of doom. To withdraw like a fly or amuse oneself
like a submarine in a fjord misnamed a canal.
To decide rain makes it worse,

but sun's bad too, but both are good.
When the answer to the question
is *die*.

When the father asks *when will we
tell the kids*, when die, when die,
when die.

Seeing the word *skull* reminds me of winter
in Santa Fe, O'Keeffe's obsession—
worn, bleached, jagged. Holy,

holey, and whole. Add: that it will never be
June in my spine. That the leaves
will return,

girls will converse, but the topaz truth went underground
with the scorpions my nephew knew where to find,
that I can't pant or paint or prance away

the traverse toward being a transient mom.
The salt of it, so not a honeycomb
of revive.

ABECEDARIAN WITH ALS

A little bit sane (a little bit not).
Blackbirds that turned out to be boat-tailed grackles.
Crows that cannot covert their fury of feathers.
Don't say Relyvrio reminds you of hemlock.
Every wave reassuringly governed by the moon, but what about riptides?
F*ck a duck!
Glad there's a joyful edge, though narrower than a willet's beak.
Hail in the forecast. A bitter taste:
it enables animals to avoid exposure to toxins.
Jaw stiffens, then relaxes. What will my body do next?
Kindness, we decide, is what we want to broadcast,
letting someone pull out in front of you in traffic,
make their turn, because the universe isn't elegant,
no one's really going anywhere important,
or running late to spin or vinyasa or
pilates. The neutral neutrons of the nucleus.
Quarks that are up, down, charm, strange, top, and bottom, though
rehab in the CD, a lunch date in Leschi, PT in Madrona—it happens.
Socrates died of centripetal paralysis, a prominent loss of sensation.
Terminal: I wish it was more like waiting out a storm with an $18 glass of pinot.
Unbound bound.
Very much looking forward to overcooked orzo and finely chopped squash.
What was that you assured me—when we die, we wake from a dream?
X marks the rear of the theater—one shove of poison—into a pure realm.
You know we're all getting off at the same exit, right?
Zooey's wish: to pray without ceasing.

I AM THE LAST LOSS,

the final constellation. I've been to Andromeda, am on my way to contemplation. The roundabout looks like a jellyfish. I'm waiting to spirit, to spin. My car, caught up in the quantum, my path lit by photons. Going toward the before. Carried weirdly, like a daughter after her father has tried and failed to choke her. Cliffs of exhaust. No end to the tremors. What are the starlings coming to? I keep getting lost. What does it mean when you sneeze three times? Vacuums and deleted edges. Silence isn't 100% magnificent but usually better than noise. It was only a matter of collide.

WHEN I'M ON THE BED

called death, I hope
to be thinking about
the texture of the bucatini
at Campiello, how they seated us
in the bar by the pizza cooks, but when we asked to sit elsewhere

they put us beside
a giant strangler fig
with fake orchids we thought were real.
Al dente, which I pronounced *al Dante*, in honor of my nephew,
in honor of the circles of hell, my heritage. When I'm on the bed called death

I hope I recall your smile that evening
when you learned *budino* means pudding,
a butterscotch pudding, which we more than managed
despite finishing our entrées. In *la stanza della morte*, shoving off
my mortal foil, may I be dreaming of butterscotch pudding, the feel of my hand

on your back, recalling the call you made
from a mile down the beach to tell me there were no
yellow hilly hoop hoops, greater cheena reenas, or frou-frou stilts.
I walk back to the car while you call again, this time to tell me you found
a flock of dunlins and semipalmated sandpipers. There's an actual flush toilet

at the parking lot! And potable water! And my love calls again,
this time to say he's nearing the path to the parking lot. No, I don't have
the keys to the car or a single coin, but I've got water, binoculars, and my phone,
a little notebook to write down the species—tricolored heron, royal tern, wood
    stork—
which I'll add to my list of what to think about when I'm on my giant bucatini
    platter of a bed.

AT THE MYCOLOGICAL SOCIETY SURVIVORS BANQUET

Dorothy Delemitrios discovered morels up Naches Pass—
*Put on your fungi goggles along streams—
you'll be stepping on them like pinecones.*

Hildegard Hendrickson revealed her passion
for matsutakes—*I stop at fifty pounds
or my back goes out!*

We were gorging on *Sparassis* noodles, drowning
in sautéed shiitakes, *Coprinus* chowder,
porcini tetrazzini.

What a great occasion to blurt out *And death
shall have no dominion,* though of course
I didn't. Instead, I continued

stuffing myself with *Boletus edulis* quiche,
asking *at what elevation, what habitat,*
all the while thinking *the mushrooms*

*to mush, this banquet to mush, each of us to mush,
though not the mighty mycelium, so long as
no one stomps or chops.*

Halfway through dinner, I couldn't stop thinking
*Of course they'll be trampled. And death
shall have no dominion?* (What was

Dylan Thomas thinking?!) Though by then they were presenting
the lifetime achievement award, the lucky *Laccaria* junkie's
name newly chiseled onto a plaque not exactly a death-

be-not-proud moment, especially when Libby Cabot leaned over,
whispered in my ear *So many've kicked after clinching*
that coveted chanterelle pin they should rename it

the Death Cap! Meanwhile, at the far end of the table,
But to scout out your very own hedgehog patch,
Jamie Notman was saying, *in a good year,*
with early rains, three harvests.

I DIDN'T UNDERSTAND KEATS'S "ODE TO A NIGHTINGALE"

until I was terminal, which when you think about it, how else are you supposed
to understand lines like *My heart aches, and a drowsy numbness pains,* or *My sense,
as though of hemlock I had drunk*? I mean, it was like the other day when I grabbed
a pillow, placed it on the red Adirondack chair in our front yard, sat there listening
to a song sparrow singing its ass off, along with a robin cheery-upping so damn much
(beyond ironic). *Some dull opiate*, indeed! Ode, schmode, I was thinking, though
I do love a praise song, am thankful and glad to proclaim that not only can I watch
two eagles copulating in the tippy-top of a western red cedar, cry because
they've found each other, are something like in love, and because earlier I saw them
doing a locked-talons flip-glide over the lake, but I can get myself out of bed,
wash my face, brush my teeth. No nightingales here in Seattle, but you get my
    approximate
drift. *Sunburnt mirth!* I totally get it, as well as *a beaker full of the warm South*,
which could be Death Valley, Cádiz, or fucking Matera! Some lady on YouTube
said Keats is drunk at this point in the poem, but my take is he's contemplating
suicide—a bubbly cocktail to snuff himself out because let's face it: being tubercular
is worse than ALS: he shook and groaned with pain, whereas all I'm dealing with
is *The weariness*, a tad of *fret*. My gray hairs aren't even shaking, but a friend
I haven't spoken to in over forty years sent me a bouquet: pink roses and purple peas!
I wonder, though, about those *viewless wings of Poesy*. Is that where we trot out
this thing called negative capability? Did he want us to figure out why poesy
is viewless, or did he want us to be uncertain? His brain is dull, as I'm sure
mine will soon be, and shit, *here there is no light* is quite the heavy, but there are
    flowers
on my table, and I remember Peggy, the red-haired girl who lived in Tofu House,
raised by her grandparents cuz she was the eighth kid in an Irish brood—her parents
done with raising kids. *Embalmed darkness*, which reminds me I need to figure out
who's doing my cremation, or maybe pony up for Recompose. I'd prefer it if the days
were shortening, if the plum tree across the street wasn't wildly bursting into bloom,
but whaddya gonna do but listen to the siskins, flickers, and jays, watch them
hop from budded-to-budded branch? We've even got these from-who-knows-where
violets cropping up in our weedy beds, along with a *murmurous haunt of flies*,

so maybe I'll stick with cremation. Yeah, I think I finally get this poem—
I was never *half in love with easeful Death*—when I thought about *my quiet breath*,
when I thought *now more than ever seems it rich to die, / To cease upon the midnight
with no pain*, cuz who the fuck wants to be in pain? Yet if I knock myself off too soon,
my family won't get that big fat check, plus no more *dee-dee-dee* of chickadees.
Uncertainly, he calls *Adieu! adieu!* I guess the nightingale's petering out,
which is also Keats's *poesy*, no? Something's buried deep, though hopefully
the music never flees, the music that is poetry.

IS THIS MY LAST FERRY TRIP?

Is this the last time I'll admire the guys
in their neon-yellow slickers, guiding us
to our parking spots before we head up

two flights to the passenger deck,
to the cafeteria where a man in a black derby
and black suspenders nods and smiles

as he nibbles popcorn? In honor of this maybe
last trip to San Juan Island, the last time
I hear that somber wail of a horn,

I'm gonna go see if there's anything I can eat,
and of course there is: Ivar's clam chowder,
just what the nutritionist ordered:

extra cream, extra butter, tiny potatoes I easily swallow.
Two spoons: one for me, one for the man
otherwise known as my personal

representative. When the time comes, he will help me administer
the cocktail that kills, but until then it's *The Marvelous
Mrs. Maisel*, his book about Vronsky and Anna,

my book about the journey to the Higgs boson,
while our daughter calls to remind us
to take pictures of things

she can draw—a sprig of rose hips, a clump of serviceberries.
A deer she nicknamed Chewy. Bellies full of chowder,
we almost forget one of us is dying.

TERMINAL SURREAL

or is it surreal terminal? Something's going on
with my mitochondria. Something to do
with oxidation. My cells

need help with ridding my body of toxins, which explains
the bear bile I drank twice daily until it turned out
it was doing nothing

but making me nauseous. Surreal swirl of feta cheesecake
topped with macerated cherries. Ooh, that tastes good.
My husband calls to tell me he just heard

the first red-winged blackbird of the season, saw bald eagles
dive-bombing mergansers. I'm just sitting here pretending
I don't have ALS, that somehow, I'll live.

Fifty degrees and partly sunny: my kind of day! To forget,
while I'm listening to honking geese, that yesterday
a friend went into hospice,

that the amount of misery is equal to or greater than the number of eggs
a termite queen will lay in a lifetime—165 million.
I learned today about the mountain stone wētā,

a cricket that, when it gets cold, freezes 85% of its body. When the blizzard
passes, it comes back to life. Meanwhile, another eagle's flying overhead,
this one solo, heading south until it's out of sight.

ABECEDARIAN ON A FRIDAY MORNING

Almost like it was, this moment, this juncture of
blood pumping from arteries, back through veins,
circling in and out of chambers, my heart's pending
demolition, like the not-for-billionaires buildings
east and west of us, like these sturdy, strapping legs
for how long strong? I walked them yesterday past
gators and a pileated woodpecker, a blue-headed vireo
hardly visible in the wax myrtle, its white-spectacled
eyes, the good news of its population on the rise.
Just before, I heard a cardinal in the cattails, the *kkkkrrrr
kkkrrr* of a little blue heron in lettuce leaves I
learn are native or introduced (fossils in Wyo-
ming and India). It's hunting for insects, fish, maybe a
North Florida hopper, a tadpole, or the elusive
Okefenokee fishing spider, who knows, or a
pig frog, which I was really hoping to see.
Questions arise throughout our deep dive into
raccoon love as four babies making high-pitched
squeaks run along the boardwalk, stopping only
to make sure their pals are still nearby, cuz no one,
us included, wants to be left alone to die. When this
vacation from the void closes shop, my lungs losing their
winsome urge to rise and fall, when I can no longer
xxx and *ooo*, even via text, breathe deep a rising moon,
yak, yap, yawn, yes, yarn, yield, or do that lub-dub thing, until
zapping myself with a cocktail that takes me where I haven't been.

SELF-ELEGIES

because why not? Why not take the smashed pinecone
of my life, render it in purple? Why not dream of baking
thirteen pies, six bumbleberry, seven sour cherry? I wouldn't
press myself into a grief box, but I will confess I'm happiest
under a sleeping sky, love the darkness like I loved to run
through old-growth Doug firs and cedars. There's no more
rolled-out crust, no more loping strides or flour, but at midnight
I read a book about microbes and fungi, how these critters
find a way into us, never leave. It's the never-leaving part
I like. It's the memory of the Cuisinart loaded with dough,
the rolling out, crimping with a fork. No grief in the night,
though I'd welcome a northern shoveler, the green head
of a mallard. The Vaux's swifts that crowd the rising moon.
My husband's favorite tomato, the Jaune Flamme.

In a Plum Village meditation, a woman says *Smile*,
so I smile, though sometimes I don't, though sometimes
I'm unable. Disabled is my smile, and a lot makes me cry.
I tell those who hear me sobbing I'm not sad, and it's true—
I'm moved when friends bring fennel soup or say I look,
well, undying, when I share my joy that my daughter
has said hello to my death, not exactly made friends with
but isn't hysterical, and isn't that like a favorite song,
the unsilence of "The Sound of Silence"? She's smiling,
beautiful in her black cap-sleeve top and oversized jeans,
and so is everything out my bedroom window. I open
my curtains to the crows, to a scrub jay in the maple.
Accepting I'll do death alone like I've done most everything:
birth, growth, forgiveness, hunger, all these freaking feelings.

The other night I danced for the first time in months
to my favorite Sheryl Crow song—opens with guitar
and drums. She sings about catching a ride, how she likes

the brochure. I used to dance on my paddleboard
for hours. Ran down all sorts of winding roads,
getting closer. I could've never walked, but I walked
for sixty-two-and-a-half years. Now I look out my window,
envy the dog walkers. Did I ever think I wouldn't be the one
jumping in? Each morning, I looked in the mirror,
said "You're sure not your grandma!" Pridefully, smugly
able. When anything went. Now the green's mostly
what I see from my wheelchair. Getting into the *done*, I guess
you'd say. A little closer to no more Polish polkas,
no impromptu kitchen waltzing. To not feeling fine.

Maybe I was stained with mercury and malathion.
Maybe that time I ran through the fog of mosquito
repellent wasn't the best idea, though we all did it,
didn't we? When a friend told me to get a watch
to keep track of my miles, I didn't know it would
become an obsession, that I would go the way
of Lou Gehrig, the Iron Horse. No one told me
don't overdo it. Even if they had, I would've been
swinging at the scallops, bashing the bivalves.
Wanna have a good cry? For decades I had flashbacks
I was having another psychotic episode. *Fear and Trembling*:
isn't that a great title? I can't blame my parents or genes
(kinda refreshing). May I free myself, like Insight
Timer instructs, of debris. May I hover like a gull.

Not sure where this is going, though, yeah,
pretty fucking sure. Pretty not pretty as my
daughter would say, kinda shapeless and no
funeral please, no roses or potted begonias.
Please donate to trolling for fish instead of
netting, to Cornell Lab of Ornithology. When
I stack breaths, I'm reminded it ceases—
that's the Hurricane Debby of this thing:
weakening diaphragmatic storms. Inhalations

de-escalating. My nineteen-year-old self didn't imagine this. I was learning bird calls, hermit thrush and song sparrow. Keeping a list, but also wandering the forest counting the decades forward, a human life like alpine snow that seems it will never melt.

III

WHEN I CAN'T GET OUT OF BED

because my cat's snoring beside me, but also not wanting to begin
the work of the day, sink scrubbing and floor sweeping,
saving bananas from fruit flies,

washing alphabet-soup spray from the microwave, I turn to the news:
that the universe "and even ourselves" are holograms,
like those rainbowy things on our credit cards.

Yes, the entire cosmos and everything in it is a rainbow, and also,
as if that's not enough, scientists can't figure out why
once two subatomic particles have rubbed electric

elbows, they never forget each other, are always in this position
they call *super*, always heads or tails, in this way forever
besties. The closest thing we have to magic,

one scientist said. Things are weirder than we ever imagined said another,
but when you think about it, it sort of makes sense
we're all the sum total of every atom

we've cavorted with. The other day I watched an irrigation sprinkler
become a rainbow in a hayfield on Best Road. Holograms?
We're a giant hologram? Well, okay,

but I still need to lecture today on the California drought,
on the tipping point, try my best to keep the band
from breaking up.

What do I tell them? That the geese are flying south. That the cat
is not both dead and alive but warm beside me,
curled into a little ball

like a bamboo basket, that she and you and I are all
every color of the rainbow, shimmering in a field
after a drenching rain.

WHAT YOU SEE ISN'T WHAT YOU GET

I was trying to make sense of Einstein's statement *God does not play dice*.
It was about measurements not being fixed. It had something to do
with probability. It was like realizing light

is both wave and particle. It was like walking on fire while eating fire,
like wearing a shirt with a wolf on it, but feeling like a wolf
in lambswool. It was like being both a crater

and a peak. Fires of unknowing. I really don't know, but gravity
pulls us, keeps us here. Apples fall from trees.
If we're sitting below one,

prepare to be bonked on the head. It's all so difficult to understand,
but Einstein was wrong, at least partly wrong: God does
play dice. It's dice all the way down. Time seems real,

right? Try again. Yet we're not hovering above our chairs.
Our mattresses stay put, as do our pontoon boats.
A mother wears her fire like a circle

of hummingbirds. The boy who won't take out the recycling
flickers like his father's shadow. Nothing
is as it appears.

IT'S DIFFICULT TO UNDERSTAND

even one of our solar system's moons. Phobos, say,
a rubble pile, with a crater six miles wide.
It orbits Mars every eight hours,

one inch closer each year, its future bleaker than most:
collide and dissipate, or collide and bequeath to Mars
a system of Saturnian rings. Phobos,

meaning fear. His twin brother, Deimos, meaning dread.
It's difficult to understand that fear and dread
are circling Mars, that both are captured

asteroids, that on Phobos I'd weigh as much as a pen
or pencil, that Deimos resembles a potato
with many eyes.

Little moons of carbon and ice. *Curiosity*
sent back footage *in real time*. Fear
passing in front of dread.

TODAY

began with a book about atoms.
The electrons are where they're
supposed to be, not somewhere else.

Began with sleep, with waking,
with a bowl of yogurt & fruit,
but before the creamy pineapple

mixed with apples & oranges, a packet
of bitter crystals dissolved in tap water,
thirty minutes to drink it down, & I did.

Today, like most days, I heard the wind
whistling. The neutrons & protons
stay in the nucleus, & the electrons,

well, they stay exactly far enough away
to not mess up the whole quantum thing.
No one knows why my motor neurons

are dying, what I did . . . though I have
my theories. Might be I didn't listen
enough to the wind, or I watched eagles fly

only when paddleboarding for hours.
Maybe I felt too much. Maybe
I overexerted? I left my emotional

umbrella in a rack, was always out there
getting pelted. Luckily, as far as I know,
terns, willets, ospreys, and gulls are immune.

WAKE-UP CALL

My first word was *duck*, bread for eager beaks.
I miss the darkness raccoons navigate
thanks to a wealth of rods and cones.

Rods and cones: we studied them in junior high.
I tried to understand but it was science fiction,
a Netflix series, like the evolution of ossicles

(primitive ears). At the Dairy Queen I ask for my mother.
I'm carrying her yoga mat, her pot of red geraniums.
I am always holding a vigil

for the Tecopa pupfish of the Mojave, extinct since 1969.
On a rare winter morning when it's not raining,
Mercury winks its eight-minute-old light.

Eight minutes! Just enough time to step in dog shit
before making my way to my car. But holy Christ,
it's good to be alive.

WHY I WANT TO BE A NOBLE GAS

Because noble gases are nonreactive, have a low boiling point.
Because they're inert, rarely involved in chemical reactions.
Because *Argon* is Greek for *idle, inactive.*
Because *Xenon* is Greek for *strange.*

Because Krypton has no idea what you mean by *recoil.*
Because Neon never tries to get even.
Because a noble gas has never
swallowed a dead fish head

dangling from the end of a lure. Because it's nice to have a narrow liquid range,
better to have a full shell of electrons than to always be seeking a few
from someone else. Because it would suck to be Sodium,
always donating its one electron to Chlorine. Because

it would also suck to be Chlorine, always stealing an electron from Sodium.
Because to be highly reactive, Francium or Cesium,
is to always need to have the last word.
Because if I were a noble gas,

I'd be the balloon floating up and away from the Screamin' Swing
and the Scrambler, the fluorescent light in my father's workroom,
the one he studied under
long into the night.

SOMETIMES IT'S NICE TO BE TAKEN AWAY

to a place like Venice Beach, where I saw a man
in a neon-green wig rollerblading while eating
spaghetti, or maybe it was ramen.

Sometimes, like Emily D. says, it's better not to be public
like a nearly-wiped-out leopard frog raised in captivity,
released into the wild. Sometimes it's better

to be a dormant spore, but okay, maybe not completely dormant,
just enough awake to read every book by Annie Ernaux.
In one she catalogs what happens at her local

superstore, including sneaking a few grapes: a *collective sense
of permission*, though to eat an entire apple
would be crossing a line,

which reminds me of alligator mamas raising their young in their mouths,
their spiky-toothed jaws, which could be a metaphor
like the line in the middle of a two-lane highway

in Upstate New York. But the spores! Scientists believe they arrived
from outer space, brought life to Earth via maybe a meteorite (?),
though how did the spore become a spore?

It doesn't get to the core of the origin story. There's no satisfaction
biting into that juicy Cosmic Crisp of why there's life
instead of just rocks, but today it feels okay

to not know. It's enough to belong to the species that stealthily scarfs
a few Bing cherries and bulk almonds, that knows a dormant spore
might be why we have spaghetti and ramen,

why I'm pedaling this fat-tire bike with a friend whose purpose
is to figure out how and why cells differentiate.
As we discuss, other humans swerve

and sing past us, some grooving to the sun, surf, and sand;
some, I'm sure, stoned on gummies, some
making videos of what it's like to be alive.

SPAS OF THE MIND

There's a spa on the outskirts of Poverty Wash,
in the mouth of a Bengal tiger,
just past the left paw

of a very elusive cloud. A most-illuminating,
cataclysm-driven, oxygen-blast spa
reinvigorates with a Cloud 9

Nirvana Espresso scrub. When I have finished
my three-hour vigilance at the base
of an authentic lava tube,

after I have bathed beside forty-two volcanic vents
in an andesitic cinder cone, I will emerge
a new woman, free from the pain

of my fragmented habitat, my non-trending misalignments.
Once, they had a treatment called *Away, Away*.
I signed up instantly.

Once, an attendant handed me a watch-paint-dry daiquiri,
an elixir concocted from a thousand stopped clocks.
My blue-horsed sanitarium

leaps through luciferase-lit rooms. Parked
beside my microcurrent resort complex:
a winged chariot housing dozens

of drowsily bobbing bioluminescent worms.
All the treatments at my health club
never expire, are 100%

non-apocalyptic, guaranteed the power of myth.
The color of my spa: the salty caramel
of a long and empty beach.

THE BUSY ROADWAYS OF THE DEAD

You were my pedal to the metal, my apple-blossomed
roadside. You made me *me*. There, in the backyard grass,
mostly weeds. Daddy, you would not be buried. No funeral for you.

You wanted to be gone, wholly gone, but you left
a highway of sad, miles of *can* and *can't*. No place to visit,
to say *Hi, Dad*, but I have this feeling the entire cosmos is yours.

How do you know that? Well, you said
you'd mess with me, and you did. No place to visit,
to pay my respects, but on the first anniversary of your death,

my phone told me it was in South Jersey, your boyhood happy place.
Oh, doesn't all growing require a little somewhere,
a little bit of thruway with not only

Aunt Jo's figs, but twelve lanes of turnpike tollbooths? In Google Docs,
I found a file named "Al's Party." It was a map
of the world. Who put it there?

No funeral, but each night I sleep knowing I don't know
what happens when we die. I really don't,
so why should I panic,

why should I think that burning a body of its matter
would contradict the law that nothing
can be created or destroyed?

CARS & SUCH

I remember my father returning from teaching at Newark State College
and taking a nap, his head propped up
on Tony the Tiger.

On his desk, a photo of Einstein with the caption *Hair: It's not the style that counts,
it's what's under it*. Before he'd change the oil in the family car,
he'd wrap a rag around his head.

Growing up, I watched him rewire a table fan into a hot-dog cooker,
and, wearing a badly sewn purple-and-orange-checkered apron
I made in Home Ec, toss pizza dough till it hit the ceiling.

I remember him standing in his kitchen at age ninety-three, holding onto the counter
to steady himself. A nurse's aide had just finishing pumping a gallon
of fluid from his lungs. My brother said *He's a Cancer. Cancers

usually die of drowning*. When his body started weeping, I thought of all the years
he held back his tears, coughed them into a tissue. We played a game
called "Mouse, mouse, get the cheese." Sitting at the kitchen table,

we'd take turns walking our little animal paws toward a plate of crackers and cheese,
grabbing one of each. When I found out he was dead, I lashed my paddleboard
to the top of my car, started backing out of the driveway. I hit the curb,

got a flat tire. How like my father to force me to slow down, make me think of him
as I waited for the mechanic outside the 76 station,
writing in my journal and weeping.

LEO

This morning I learn a new constellation. It's near Venus,
to the right of Ursa Major. Visible from anywhere,
says Space.com, so why had I never seen it?

Between Cancer and Virgo, the sign between me
and my father, which made sense in a 4:45 a.m.
kind of way,

the way planets and grief might simmer together in a broth,
might pull at each other's ankles. I was in bed,
reading a book about a fox and a deer

taking revenge on a hunter. Isn't Orion a hunter? But I didn't see Orion.
I don't think my father knew about Leo, its three spiral galaxies
thirty-five million light years away,

its primordial gas cloud six times wider than the Milky Way.
All that time together, neither of us knowing
a lion was prowling above and between us.

WHEN MY PHONE TELLS ME

it's in South Jersey, halfway between
my father's favorite sister's grave
and the Santaniello farm

where he told me he was happiest.
When my phone, each time
I log in, sends a message

that someone in South Jersey's
logging into my phone,
I call AppleCare.

Am I being hacked? No, I'm assured.
But I'm in Seattle. It's my phone,
but not where I am,

on the first anniversary of my father's death,
my phone between the farm in Rocky Hill,
where my father milked cows,

ran through fields when his asthma forced him
out of Brooklyn. How many times
did he tell me *Your Aunt Glor*

and me—well, blood is thicker than water.
How many times that his best year
was the one with his Uncle Tony,

away from the soot of the city, from his father's
fruit truck, the bar where he tapped
his first keg at the age of six?

WHY I'D MAKE A GREAT CHEMIST

Because my father was the X in $X +\text{-}e \rightarrow X\text{-} +$ energy.

Because my sister knits plutonium sweaters.

Because none of my valence shells will ever fill.

Because I love figuring out what all the arrows point to.

Because speaking of shells, let me share with you some of my favorites: angel wing, horse mussel, knobbed whelk.

Because even though I misread *ionization* as *intoxication*, I'm sober as a lab mouse.

Because lighting a Bunsen burner is the first step in creating an altar.

Because I also misread *atomic radii* as *aromatic radii*, dreamt a giant composite radiating orange peel and rhyme.

Because I could get serious about electron affinity, especially dressed in a powder-blue frock.

Because I'm always stepping away from the hood to look up words like *mercurial*.

Because nothing I'm fond of will function at standard pressure and temperature.

Because I understand how Marie Curie spent all those painstaking hours weighing pitchblende.

Because I try not to revel but I revel, shattering (sorry!) every pipette within a hundred-mile radius.

Because even though the elements are more like friends I want to dance the Macarena with, I swear my allegiance to the Copernican principle.

Because "to solve" derives from the Latin *solvere*: to loosen, untie, release.

Because solving's just another word for letting go.

IV

JOHN MUIR ELEMENTARY

When John Muir said *Nature's peace will flow into you
as sunshine flows into trees*, he could not have imagined

John Muir Elementary, nondescript brick surrounded
by asphalt, a playground where ropes dangle from poles

lacking tetherballs. Could not have been thinking,
when he declared *All that the sun shines on is beautiful*,

of the bark chips, the chain-link fence, the twenty-minute
daily allotment of recess, the cafeteria ladies serving up

USDA surplus beef to the 75% who qualify for free lunch.
Oh, John! I'm sure you'd have an issue with the downer cows

they feed our nation's youth, cows the district buries
in a far-off place. John! No grass, no dirt, though okay,

two California redwoods over by the fading hopscotch boards,
trees where my daughter plays hide-and-seek with Heaven

and Daejah, Camille, and Cerrell—*Camille* like *com'ere, Cerrell*
like *surreal*, which is what it is when the principal struts outside

with her megaphone, tells us if this was an actual fire
we wouldn't have burned, commending us for exiting quickly

from the library where we were deeply ensconced in *The Wild Muir*.
Come to think of it, John, I think you'd be pleased it bears your name.

Who knows? Your ghost might be cozying up to the backstop
and the blackboards, looking on as the playground monitor greets

the hijab-ed, the braided, and the cornrowed. It's not real brick.
There's no veggie or native plant garden, but if you show up

59

on Talent Night, Heritage Night, Math Night, or the End-of-Year Potluck, the kindergartners will be on stage belting out "What a Wonderful World."

They will hear you clapping from across the rainbow bridge, because, like you said, *We all flow from one fountain Soul.*

NEXT WEEK WE HAVE A DOUDLE ASSINMENT

I'd written at the bottom of a crayon drawing
of a house with a chimney, a wisp
of blue smoke. Next week,

the Sunday school teacher warned us, prepared us.
I wonder what those two assignments were:
Christ's death and resurrection? Coveting

your neighbor and their wife? I was nine, still
a believer. I hadn't yet asked my father
(*Don't ask me cuz I don't know*).

I enjoyed Sunday school, didn't miss at all the long,
boring sermons I never listened to
because I was writing

long sentences in cursive on the ceiling beams,
counting how many parishioners wore glasses.
My sister taunted me for my bad spelling:

Doudle? What's a Doudle Assinment? Was I doubting
being assigned sin? I got better and better at spelling,
which is maybe the only upside of shame,

better and better at questioning faith, questioning a man in the sky
always watching. Now I know God is a placeholder word
for not a man but a hunch, a feeling,

a stand-in for a concept no two people share. I don't believe,
do I? But I know how low the odds of atoms, at the birth
of the cosmos, not breaking apart,

of gravity not too strong and not too weak. I know there are 17,500 species
of butterflies—is their sole purpose to pollinate, to be eaten by warblers,
orioles, grosbeaks, jays, tanagers, mockingbirds? To be gobbled up

by lizards and snakes, frogs and wasps, monkeys and rats?
Where does it derive from, this thing we call a food chain,
this intricate web, which, of course, leads me to spiders,

the webs I break on the way to my car, beside clumps
of raggedy oxeye daisies. Every sunrise.
Every giraffe tongue, each warthog

tusk, each stiff tuft of a billy goat's laughable beard. All this time
to bring me here, across from Red Apple Market, a breeze lifting
the sycamore leaves, their shadows enlivening the sidewalk.

THERE ARE THOUSANDS OF PLEASURES,

thousands of ways to not be dissatisfied, to not embrace the terms
of anxiety. One of them is to consider the length
of a giraffe's tongue: twenty-one inches.

Another is to go in pursuit of blackberries only a person in a boat
can reach. It's important to be responsive to tails and ears,
to limbs that allow you, domestic cats, and gazelles

to lope toward Ladybug Espresso or a rat. Away
from a charging hippo. It's better to light
a sparkler than to whine, right?

It is better to thank your body for its heels, its ability to heal.
That although they are dreadlocked and devoted,
you are not a Bergamasco sheepdog. To avoid

a sort of manic obsession with less-than, stare at the pinking clouds
longer than seems appropriate. Way longer. To gloss your brain,
revel in the long-ago-ness of your past, focus mostly

on the gigantic-peach present that really does take up most of the fridge.
When you spot a plate of envy, take a sniff, decide to pass.
Your eyes are infinite. So is the number of beetles

in the tropics. Choose your path like you're choosing a stallion,
pick carefully through the leaves of spinach, careful
not to harm the baby slugs.

You are that baby slug. You are that minute that sometimes feels like an hour
and sometimes feels like a nanosecond. Gather up all your dusty doubts,
put them in the Ridwell bin.

Know they will be recycled into something useful,
like a park bench. Kneel at least once a day,
preferably at dusk, preferably

in front of someone or something that sustains you,
a bed of bok choy, a cantaloupe,
a trembling elm.

DOUBLE TRIPTYCH FOR THE MONTHS OF NECTARINE AND PLUM

1

She wants to be buried, says *Put more here*,
and when I do, *I like it*.

I can't even run, she says, and she's right.
Finds a worm, but it flies away.

2

She and her brother say they hate
flowers, don't want to visit

a stupid garden, want to climb, slide,
spin, swing, anything but confinement

in a swirl of stonecrop, chicory, delphinium.
But then they see the playhouse, meet the kid

to hide from, see the rough-winged swallow
squeezing into a nest box, the day turns

woodruff, rosemary, Japanese lilac.

3

She wanted to be X, then O, then X.
She wants a bite of plum, to share
the plum.

Then the horse's bell, the sound
of breathing horse, the breeze,
a kingfisher's call,

the plum in her hand all her own.

4

"My nectarine is singing," she says.
What's it singing, I ask.
"Mary had a little lamb,"
and "Life is but a dream."
Does it dance?
"No, it just sings."

5

"My favorite color's either
black, sparkly green, brown, no,
green, no, blue, no, you can't
brush my hair, privacy, I need you,
put me down, go sit over there,
don't leave."

6

This morning each child
claimed half of me. Divided
down the middle by my jacket zipper,

I lay on the Marmoleum. "Keep to your side!"
they took turns screaming.
Then one would fall off, complain

they didn't have enough room, that the other
had more, that they needed to go past my jacket zipper
just a little to balance things out.

Each with their own piece of a mommy
who wondered which piece was her own.

KEY GROVE

    after a sculpture by Clark Wiegman

Why keys?
I didn't ask myself
all those years I lived

down the street
from a grove of them.
When my daughter was six, I brought her

to the not-grove,
to a concrete walkway
in front of our local high school.

Girl that she was,
she asked me to lift her up,
let her sit inside the one with the biggest bow.

There she held her pink puppy.
There she yelled *Mama, I'm in a key!*
There, where it seemed she would always be solvable.

The key to my _____.
The key to her _____.
The answer key. Answers to every problem.

The dry winged fruit
of ashes and maples is a samara,
but also a key, song in the key of life, but I could not

key into, but I was off-key,
not a key figure, more a low-lying reef.
A word with unknown origins, with an abnormal

evolution, no sure cognates
other than *kei* and *keinan* ("to germinate").
Was there a key moment? When had it clicked?

On a spring day eleven years later
I went back. Nine keys, no two alike.
Bushtits in a nearby tree, a singing finch.

What do they open?
Not the irises in the bed beneath.
Not the bedstraw or the sky, not the mouths

of the students who wear their masks
on their chins, not the crow that stands
on a garbage can, the starling that pecks the stairs.

A set of keys could be helpful. Crucially
important. A key with all the right answers. Cattywampus
keys. There are no keys. I tried them all. Nothing unlocked.

HOW IT IS TODAY

Woke up not smiling but grateful to walk
to the bathroom, wash my face.
Grateful my daughter

wants to help. A Bewick's wren singing
outside my window, hello
from out there

where I cannot go, though will try to later
when I've taken half a Ritalin,
which gives me four hours

of relative pep. Yesterday we saw two juvenile eagles,
a chestnut-backed chickadee, stopped at a bench
where I did my five-part breathing

while feeling the cool breeze through lakeside willows.
Thankful, so thankful, my bestie's in the kitchen,
brewing me tea, icing it to cool my throat,

sore from talking, the luck of talking, of every-three-hour hunger
fed. Anxiety, I forgive you. As I face my fears in a pair
of loose-fitting pants with light blue

and yellow flowers, my needs becoming clearer—
hugs, naps, my daughter's yam soup—untangling
the feelings like the mess of cords beside my bed.

WHAT I DIDN'T REALIZE

before I was terminal
wouldn't fit in the red plastic bowl
we often fill with rippled potato chips.

I hadn't considered someone might use up
their last couple years planning their memorial,
right down to the poems and songs. I mean, it might be nice

to know someone will get up and recite Neruda's
"Through a closed mouth the flies enter," but actually
I prefer taking the world's slowest walk, where I hear coots

making their high-pitched calls
that remind me they need each other,
need to be in tight formation, cuz otherwise

an eagle has a better chance
of swooping down, carrying one of them off
in its talons. I'd rather be gaga about the sun,

that it's actually sunny,
embracing what, by 1 p.m., will be rain,
that feeling I get out here when I hear the ticking of a hummingbird.

HOW TO FALL

Prioritize not bashing your noggin—that makes good sense
cuz hitting it could be deadly. You don't want
a secret bleed inside that

sweet skull of yours, right? If it looks like you're taking it
from the top, for God's sake turn your head
to one side. Aim to teeter sidelong,

not onto your back, which can really mess you up. Also,
it's a good idea, as you careen, to make
like a twirly bird. As the Bible

and the Byrds song say: *Turn! Turn! Turn!* There is a season
for running without tripping, and then there's
loose carpets, a backpack left in the middle

of the floor. Jeez, kids, please don't drop your slides
in the path from the kitchen to the front door—
do you want your mother

to break her arms and wrists? It says stay loose. I get it,
but isn't it hard to relax when you've tripped,
don't know what's happened

or how it will end? A website suggests rolling out of it,
I guess like you're playing in the surf, in and out
of waves that never slap or hurt.

It's like they think we have complete control of our tumbles,
our foibles, our faults, but the question is: do we?
Spread out the impact is another tip.

I think this means the love of family and friends, an Olympic-size pool
of folks who bring you chocolate pudding, homemade soy milk,
potato-leek soup. What you want

is a squatting position, legs over your head,
a great deal of momentum from this life
into the next.

AFTER DROPPING MY SON OFF AT COLLEGE,

I sit in my hotel bed watching a video of a condor
flapping its wings on a cliff edge. Facing away,

turning toward a crowd singing
its high-pitched song of digital cameras

clicking, as they wait for the condor to soar.
It turns around two, three, a dozen times to those

who raised it, flaps a few times more, bows
to the cheering and clapping, uplifting music

queued as the condor alights, lands on a boulder
below. And now I'm in a Starbucks off I-5,

reading about this bird that traveled with the bison,
whose fossils have been found in New York,

the range of a single bird the size of Maryland:
fifteen thousand miles. I watch again a condor spread

its wings, spread and retract, raise its bill into
the uncertain air, tip forward, take flight.

POEM ON MY SON'S TWENTY-THIRD BIRTHDAY

How far away it seems, I told him last night, over rainbow rolls and agedashi.
How I went into labor on a Wednesday. Three days of people saying
I wasn't, that it was weeks away. On Saturday, I called the doula.

She suggested we go to the zoo. Three hours later he was slipping out of me
like a five-pound bass. Wide-eyed and curious,
he took a good look at us. Then he cried,

went for my breast. I didn't know how tired and anxious I'd get, how sure
someone would call CPS, how I'd panic when I couldn't stop his crying
even while belting out "Maxwell's Silver Hammer."

The night I ended up at Behavioral Health, my son in a squad car
because I said I wasn't sure, when they asked,
if I'd hurt him.

It was October. We'd pasted black bats on our front door,
strung candy-corn lights. I began hearing crows
that weren't there. Little boy in his blue fleecy.

Your dad brought you each afternoon during visiting hour,
where I held you, not sure I'd ever get out. My now
was committed. My mind, though doing better,

had spent a week hearing my father in the hallway, believing God,
the Unabomber, and I were in cahoots. But it turned out
to be hormonal. Soon I was taking him to mom

and baby yoga. We had a little routine, me-n-you: mornings on the go,
then home for your nap, then playing in the backyard, which morphed
to museums and zoos, to preschool

and school, two graduations, to this day I'm not telling you,
as I'm placing twenty-three candles on your cake, I spent four weeks
away from you because they thought I'd kill you.

Because I thought I was smoldering in a can like the ones they filled with wood,
set on fire beside a frozen Tommy's Pond.
What did that month end up mattering?

Less than this sip of sake I drink from your cup, less than this dab of wasabi
on my hamachi, less than this moment,
which leads to the next.

MY NINETEEN-YEAR-OLD DAUGHTER IS MY PERSONAL ASSISTANT,

learning what I need, what I need most. What I'm paying her for
mostly is having her in my arms, stroking her hair
because I don't know how much longer.

Is bringing me overnight oats with a dollop of yogurt,
a few smashed raspberries on top, with a label
that says I LOVE YOU in red marker.

Is watching three episodes of *Girls*, trying to decide
which character we like most—Hannah or Shosh,
or maybe Hannah's boyfriend Adam,

whom we hated at first (he peed on her in the shower!),
but who, by the end of Season 2, seems way less gross
and full of himself, wisdom-y

about romantic love. Is bingeing on rom-coms
with formulaic plots that always end
with a car, boat, or plane chase

to tell the woman *I love you*, which always makes me cry,
but a good kind of cry, ya know? Is when she asks
for a list of tasks, and at the top is *Come say hi*,

and tell me how you are (sweeping and mopping be damned!).
Is *Sit with me on the chaise*, listening to a scrub jay,
though we cannot see it,

though we don't know exactly where it is, how long
it will be there doing its weirdly scratchy
yet somehow melodious call.

A POEM ABOUT TWINFLOWER

because my daughter says it's her favorite flower.
Because the blooms smell sweet—pale pink,
nodding bells. Because it grows

in moist, shady woods. Because the inflorescence
is trumpet-shaped like a pair of dangly earrings.
That she and I are paired too.

That being her mother is not to be her twin
but to be, at times, her creeping vine,
her comfort mat

of evergreen. That it grows in the mountains, the hikes
to Buckhorn Lake and Constance Pass,
where we found them beneath

hemlock and silver fir, among starflower,
lupine and pentstemon, heart-leaved arnica.
Where we pitched our tents,

where during the night we saw Jupiter, Saturn, and Mars.
Because this flower reminds me we will always
be dangling from the same stem,

that mothers and daughters are perennial. Blooming all summer,
dormant under snow, returning each June,
alongside club moss and deer fern,

in the cool dark forest where her body's half her father's,
half mine, but also all hers, where long-running stems
adhere us to the fragrant ground.

SPOON THEORY

First text of the day: *Mama: Only 12 spoons a day.*
Let me see: four spoons for a two-mile walk
on the beach, seeing a family of dolphins

several laughing gulls, two Forster's terns.
Another two spoons for ten minutes
of gentle yoga. Already halfway

there by noon, but before that I got out of bed (1), dressed (1),
took meds (1), made egg salad, boiled water for pasta
(3 more!), and then I showered—two more.

Throughout, I checked social media (2), graded a dozen sonnets (2 more?!).
So, now I'm at sixteen spoons, without counting packing a suitcase
and backpack, reading a book about muons, gluons, positrons,

and quarks, sending and answering a bunch of emails and texts.
I guess it's naptime? I guess it's takeout for dinner
and a little TV, which may keep me

under twenty-four? What my daughter wrote: *Embrace the coziness and stillness of life.* What I did: stood in front of a ninth-floor window in Warrior 3,
then settled into tree pose.

SMILE

because you're alive, not yet paralyzed. Smile because a pair of eagles
with bright white heads and rumps just flew over your house,
because you can hear the sound of your son's feet

on the side-porch stairs. Smile because there's blended peanut butter,
strawberry jam your daughter left in the fridge—slippery good.
Because you can bundle up in your purple parka,

your pink pom-pom hat, sit on your deck on a sunny afternoon
knowing your megadose of vitamin B12, the latest
ALS-symptom slow-down, is on its way

from a pharmacy in Hopewell, New Jersey. Freaking *Hopewell*,
where the pharmacist sounds like any one of your high school
bestie's moms—*Honey, cawl me with the insurance info*

when you're back from your wawk. Because smiling begets happiness,
smile at the lichen on the bark of a small Doug fir on the trail
overlooking the harbor, because soon, very soon, maybe

this summer, there'll be a drug that doesn't slow symptoms but reverses them,
because your sister texted *If you put your left hand on your heart,*
your right hand on a tree, you're in sync.

IF WE DIDN'T LEAVE THE TASK TO BACKHOES

The weather is a bright and obvious song. It's noon before you realize
you've spent three hours freshening the herb pots,
feeding the ornamentals Miracle-Gro,

listening to a towhee, its wacky, off-kilter song, deciding it's time
to dig a giant hole for a root-bound hydrangea.
The earth is stubborn, doesn't want

to be messed with, so you change from sandals to sneakers,
put your full weight onto the shovel's rim
as your mind wanders to the uncle,

cousins, and brothers who took turns digging your mother's grave.
Talk about a cross-cultural experience! Anyone digging
anyone's grave. A task that has united,

would continue to unite, if we didn't leave the task to backhoes.
The expression: *digging your own grave.*
Freedictionary.com says

it's being responsible for your own ruin. When your son
was young, you took him to a Day of the Dead exhibit
at the Burke Museum. Sugar skulls,

all order of marigolds. Dioramas of cultural practices from around the world.
One about a society requiring its men to dig their own graves.
Not prisoners of the Nazis or ISIS,

just a guy in a country where part of the deal is to foster a clear sense
of one's future, regardless of being one's worst enemy,
of shooting oneself in the foot.

Twenty minutes to dig a one-foot hole. A feeling of victory
when the plant fits perfectly, and I tamp the dirt
into place.

LEGACY

If I'm lucky
for a few generations
some of my kin
will be trying
to figure me out

*She sure could cackle
and guffaw whip up
a tasty confession pie
always let me lick the spoon*

Very lucky since
I have no idea
who this Bullock woman was
mother of my great-grandmother
Pickarski who was mother
to my grandma Katrosh

Very lucky if my children
have children
though I won't hold
or raspberry them
say *the coat says cold*

who will tell their kids
how I scarfed mashed potatoes
directly from the serving bowl
how I taught them how to flip
how not to fear the blob monster

I cherished a collection
of miniature plastic saints
though won't go down
as an expert in hospital corners

utensil sorting picking up
a jug of laundry soap at Costco
keeping my hair neatly coiffed

If I'm very very lucky
my grandchildren will tell
their daughters and sons
about a feisty feckful gal

who fancied words like *gherkin*
and *scintillate* who shouted *bearded
lizard on the loose!* Reveled
in proverbs and fables
in blabbing stuff like *O' foggage green!
An' cranreuch cauld!* in saying
as opposed to not

V

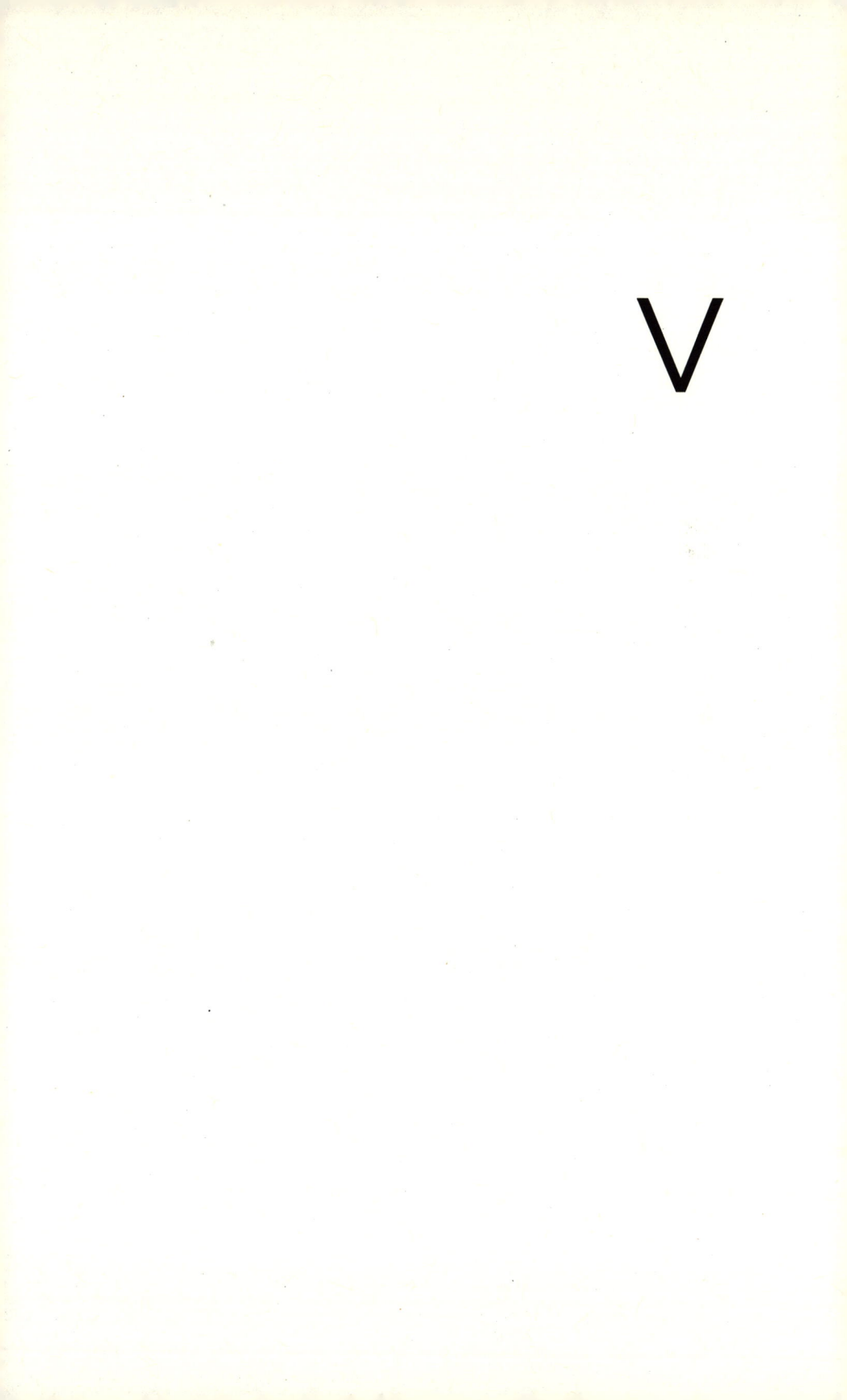

I FOUND SMALL SLICES OF JOY

at the local swamp
at what used to be
a cement factory
now a series of paths
for mothers pointing
to herons and thrushes

I found a slice of joy
in the puddled path
in a cherry tree
with a spotted towhee
watching students watch
a sparrow in a cottonwood

There was a slice of joy
just hidden enough to take a pee
privacy in the ivy not too close
to a ratty blue tent
another slice when I heard a marsh wren
saw the white breast of a violet-green swallow

I ALWAYS WAKE UP HAPPY

because, you know, I could've died while I lay me down.
Plus, I'm not van Gogh, that bipolar genius
who cut off his ear when Gaugin left Arles.
Dang, he didn't know

how brilliant he was: no one did. Even after he painted
The Starry Night, which I just looked up,
and it's worth 100 million dollars,
but really we all know

it's priceless. Imagine what he could've done with that money then—
paid back his brother Theo, repainted The Yellow House,
given each of his favorite whores a million-dollar tip.
But I'm not him: a loose end, a lose end—

even at my worst I'm a resting cedar in the hour of deer and raindrop.
Even at my worst, the streetlamp stays lit all night,
the steam rises from the kettle, and my daughter
pours herself a cup of English Breakfast.

Nothing's unrelenting. It's pretty much all a dark chocolate bar
with salted almonds. The landscape is lily pads
with unbothered bees. If there's flight,
the plane lands with barely a bump.

But van Gogh. He attained but didn't know it.
How sad is that. He was a wood dove
without a wood, a pond without
a reflection. Boughs

without a tree. I could go on. It's misty and forlorn over there
in the Midi. The rainy cold is different there,
as is the tea, which is kind of the color
of lunacy, what they used to call it,

a tea that drowns gnats. I always wake up happy,
imagining van Gogh at Saint Paul de Mausole
asylum, madly painting olive groves
and poplars.

TAKING A WALK WITH RIMBAUD

Someone's bidding on the Eat Ship and Dive;
someone's betting the body will surface,
the perilous viper won't bite.

At the Joseph Cornell retrospective, I was surprised the clay pipe
blew soap bubbles at the moon. We were in Paris,
cannonballing into the Seine.

Oh, Rimbaud, did you know you were charming?
Hold on, and God the mixologist
will fix you a Black Death.

Someone's bidding on the Far Niente. Something rid us
of our grand jeté, our invincible schtick,
our Jupiter bliss.

POSTCARD FROM SOME UNKNOWN
PART OF MY BRAIN

that may be missing an enzyme. Missive from *I believed*
my version of ruse and ruin. It's true: at boulevards I seek out
the craziest donuts, Bear Mountain Bavarian, Triple Blitz Crunch.
Everywhere I turn, the tulips are redder than the Spanish word

for blood. Everywhere the curbs are crumbling (don't go barefoot).
Everywhere: prosecco fountains empty into cruise-able rivers.
I want the dead to be what pops when I shake the bottle,
aim the cork at the hedges. What I promise is the tenderness

of a tamed tiger, a small gray cat crawling under your duvet.
Did you say *permission* or *persimmon*? Either way,
I will be your plankton, what keeps you phosphorescent.
Together let's venture into imperishable brightness,

dimness suddenly strobing. Find a seat beside a bed
of crocuses, which you'll remind me is where we get saffron.
Dine on and shine on. Become more than a chainsaw
and its log. At our feet the space junk of the '60s and '70s,

scraps of the lunar module that carried Neil and Buzz.
It's true: I get mean when I don't get my way, when I'm forced
to build a nest in the future tense, when I'm forbidden
the call of an osprey. When heat gives way to dusk.

WHAT I'LL MISS

prob won't be sycamores, a childhood of nesting robins,
peeling bark. Will it be the bald cypresses at Corkscrew Swamp,
the last three miles of a thirty-mile swath saved from chopping and draining,

conversion to *crop or pasture use*? I know I'll def miss
the return of the swallows to Seattle on or about March 18th,
the violet-greens, their acrobatic flights along and across the lake.

Also, though I don't love the smell it burrows into my fleece,
the flames of a campfire along the Tieton, though let's skip the s'mores.
I'll miss walking, I think, unless what we do without bodies is more like a kestrel

in a dragonfly divebomb. If we fly,
and I think we will, I'll have to go back to that suburb
outside Townsville to revisit the duck-billed platypus who showed up

on our final morning while I was washing our sleeping bags
in our world-peace hosts' front loader, preparing for four more months
of hostels, bamboo huts, and pullout couches. Do I have to say I won't miss

tooth or hair care, those days the AQI nudged past 300,
the mornings of building towers out of yogurt and ricotta containers
when I would've much rather been jogging, swimming, or lying in a hammock?

Yes, yes, we will all fly, and the years flew
like a crested caracara just before the turnoff to the last old-growth stand
of bald cypress in the world. Yes, yes, the word is caress, and I will miss doing it

with you, and also monkeys and featherless chicks,
owls right before they upchuck this thing called a pellet—
the bones and the fur, which I also plan to savor, the gristle

and the chewy fat, the parts my father ate
so my sister and I could have the filet mignon,
which I sort of did the same for my kids (?), those nestlings

who fledged, those neotropical migrants who landed
on 33rd Avenue South, with their many markings—confusing
stripes, eye-rings, and so many permutations of yellow throats.

I WANT TO BE AN ADIRONDACK CHAIR

dusted with browning plum and cherry blossoms.
I want to be outside on all days, in all weather,
to never have to go inside, choose a cookbook,

a recipe, plug in the rice cooker, peel the yams, sharpen
the knife. I want to be in earshot of the juncos
and chickadees, of the Steller's jay

with its punk-rocker crest, as if it had been dipped
in Extreme Blue. I want to have a front-row seat
when the neighbor's paper gets delivered

at 4 a.m. I could say I want to be the mauve-leaved maple,
or the streetlight, or the dead-end sign, but really
what I want is to be a thing people sit on,

take a load off, a place where there's just enough sun. Where,
perhaps, the mail carrier will stroll by, hand a someone
coupons and circulars, but not divorce papers,

shutoff notices, a summons for jury duty. If I could be
an Adirondack chair, I'd stop complaining
about the crumbs on the counter,

the floor, the stairs. I'd be out here, beside the blooming lavender,
so the dried mud on the hardwood floors wouldn't matter;
I'd be overhearing my neighbors

loading their bicycles onto their car, debating whether to take I-5
or Highway 99, one reminding the other to clamp down
the tires, *cuz you know what happened*

last time. If I were wooden, if I were painted red, I swear I'd stop
wishing I was paddling when I'm running, running
when I'm paddling. I'd just be happy

where I am, out in the front yard, admiring my favorite feline
as she reduces a German shepherd
to a whimpering mess.

SHE'S PRETTY MUCH WHO SHE WAS,

that woman with her head in a book about the Higgs boson,
that lady petting her cat Nacho, the dilute tortie tabby
who, when you ask her if she wants to go outside,

meows *yes*. That mama loving her children
like banana splits with extra peanuts,
like an all-day paddleboard trip

to the I-90 bridge and back, though hold the peanuts,
hold the paddleboard, hold the bananas unless
they're chopped into very small pieces,

added to the overnight oats she eats in her bed
so she doesn't have to walk downstairs
cuz she's hypermetabolic, always,

always tired. She did eat salmon last night
from the Copper River, but mostly
she's downing shakes

and smoothies, mostly she sits on a chaise in her front yard,
waiting for a hummingbird to stick its beak
into a magenta flower she doesn't know

the name of cuz it isn't native. Waiting for a kinglet's
whistle, the sound of her husband's car
pulling into a driveway, the music

of his tires on concrete slats. All day a kind of waiting for dinner,
after which she can shower, do a few cat-cows, one
down dog, a thirty-second one-leg stand on each leg,

a one-block walk. Pretty much who she was, minus
the long runs in the woods, minus the hikes
to places like Sunrise and Paradise.

YOU-N-ME

In your world it's all coming up trumpets: mushrooms and swans.
In my world there's a place where a drum set used to reside.

Your world's a jacuzzi with five working jets.
My world's a plumber who called in sick.

You're rife with uncaptivity.
I've got the heavy-metal guitar solo of a howler monkey in a cage.

For me, it's kind of a button I need to sew back on a black coat.
A frayed hem. A mouthful of pins.

For you, the dress is not only in the bag,
it has no dirty laundry up its sleeve.

Me? Cooing pigeons. All damn day.
You? Something sonorous—a wood thrush on a green-leaved branch.

I'm tired of my shade, the unwieldy camellia, the hedges wailing
Trim Me! I feel like the grass that died when we put up the trampoline.

You're wide awake in a back-country tent, studying your atlas, map, and GPS.
I'm a female mallard in winter plumage: don't try to find me in the reeds.

I'm the laptop unauthorized to play "Sweet Home Alabama."
You're the Simon and Garfunkel reunion concert in Central Park.

While I wait for the sofa bed to arrive, for the guests who keep
inviting more guests, you shoot me a quick text: *On my way to SF!*

In your world, the living see the entire spectra. Crazy-ass colors,
lurple and *fagenta*. My world's a cloudy day in Tacoma.

It's all good, we say. It all comes out in the wash,
but your rug's psychedelic, and mine has a stain that won't lift.

POETRY,

they said. Focus like a plank of wood stays focused
on the plank it rubs against, the nails,
on the warping as they age. Stay

creative. Like others, create. Flourish like a leaf leafing,
like a Kentucky spring, like the network in a stem.
Let your brain be French or Guyanese, create

un-dreading routines. In place of late trains, place mountains
and Ferris wheels in your dreams. Motivational quotes,
like *Look as carefully at yourself*

as you do the sun. Cultivate the unexpected like cultivating
plums. Become the uncommon prune of the ages.
Find a new word for *walls*. Focus

on Planck's constant, on the quark known as *charm*.
Try having your best lifetime, though a Guinness
is fine, a cocktail with a hibiscus base.

Be the antidote and the anecdote. Force books and windfall apples
onto your besties, six-foot clams and fossils of camels from here
to Spokane. Reverse adversity while confronting arthritis

of the mind. Enough is not always enough. Call it
an independence growing less ominous
across the Midwest, something akin

to the Saint Louis Arch. Especially in the morning,
listen to mourning doves and scientists. Endurance
is within your gasp. Outside Austin,

pop your lines, make them go feather, un-rust.
Let your noggin weirden: it helps. Each of us,
like an apron or an albatross,

has a back and front. X out judgment. Your theater
is a doorway: improve on what can be improved,
on a little strategic wandering

beyond the recipe. Limit the part of you that doesn't want
to be a child. Unrigid your flagpole. Sharp can be bad
but also works, the zeitgeist in your kombucha.

Mine nonoperatic projects. Be the movie that ends
with a bright black beetle. Don't let social media
tailor your musings, though let it if it will.

Except when you're not, be a language economist. Let passion
be your business, 9 to 9. Your reward? Handstands,
an open-ended stylus, singing by the pound.

PORTRAIT OF APPLE CINNAMON MUSH, CHOBANI YOGURT DRINK, AND BIPAP

that states on the readout I had 4.6 events per hour.
I think this means I stopped breathing
an average of almost five times

an hour. Not because my lungs are weakening (yet)
but the stuff near my lungs, like my diaphragm.
I'm grateful for this machine that forces air

in and out of me, that it's on the lowest setting,
that to keep it insured I only have to use it
four hours a night, and also

that a northern flicker just called from a big-leaf maple,
that a cat is at my feet, sorta like she knows what's up
with not only my lungs but my sedentary self.

Grateful for Xanax, cuz what did people do without
antianxiety meds? Love that it's a palindrome!
On the day my husband pointed this out,

it was a clue in that day's *NY Times* crossword puzzle.
Grateful it's cloudy, so it feels a little better
spending so much time in bed (so much

harder when the sun shines through the curtains—believe me).
For a book titled *The Sound of a Wild Snail Eating*,
about a bedridden woman who finds comfort

in watching a snail sleep most of the day, then munch
on a portobello mushroom all night. Cuz basically,
without Ambien, I'd be that snail.

BEFORE AND AFTER: A QUASI-ABECEDARIAN

Once I thought like an aardvark; now, I think like an ant.
Once I was a ribbon; now I'm a big red bow.
Once I was a crimson chat; now I'm a condor.
Dogs bark at my door; together, we dance.
Everything is electric with ease. There is no edge.
Before, failure was my face.
I was a garden of grief.
In the halftime of my life, I'd sipped misery's mist.
I was the inch-long inchworm, slowly increasing.
I was a jailed jewel.
My kayak almost tipped; my luck limped.
The macaque of my heart would not mend.
Nobody knew it, but I was a nervous nightjar.
My secret pain, tidal, like an ocean,
pain like saw palms waving in the cold:
my whole life a pop quiz
when the rain went river, went roar.
Suddenly, sadness sailed away on a sloop.
My tarnished teakettle glowed.
My ugly and useless umbrella blew away.
My vexing vamoosed, a long vacation to Valencia.
What window had I climbed through?
The window of exuberance.
You can find it too . . .
all you have to do is loosen the zipper of fear.

MAKING THE BEST OF IT

Today I learned Keats was only five feet tall. *A compact corpse*
says Di Suess in "Romantic Poetry," *shorter than Prince,*
which I so love knowing, along with the fact

a Steller's jay might imitate the call of an osprey, line its nest
with pine needles or fur. Fur! That a Pacific geoduck
can live for over 160 years.

I interrupt my reading husband, share the news of a clam
weighing three pounds, that its neck is *baseball length,*
so to eat one you really need to dig deep,

down to armpit depth. As I lose my ability to breathe,
as walking becomes a rare treat, as I wake at 3 a.m.
in painful positions, perplexed by my body's

next move, I'm delighted by the drawing of a pigeon guillemot,
to learn of its bright red feet, the zing of chartreuse
hiding under Oregon grape's bark,

the six pale-gray eggs of the great blue heron, that strange,
screechy call of a bald eagle in my neighborhood.
On warm days an Anna's hummingbird buzzes

near the chaise I rest on. Black-headed grosbeaks
that wintered in freaking Mexico sing
in a big-leaf maple

as I text my daughter what Di said: *What doesn't die?*
The closest I've come to an answer
is poetry.

YOU ARE MUCH MORE THAN THIS BODY
Thích Nhất Hạnh

which is really good to know because these days
this body isn't the electric eel it once was, isn't
sputtering like bacon or fizzing like a Coke,

is more like a salt lick without the salt, a bunch of wasps
on a vacation from buzzing. I'm no longer busy
like sugar ants in a left-out-by-mistake

tin of Fussie Cat, but I'm learning to notice lichen (wildly
chartreuse), the trunks of madrone, their breast-ish
protuberances. Also, a bush with both berries

and buds, and I liked that news—that we could be done fruiting,
last season's puckered maroon, but also, check it out,
little green shoots! I liked the way the wind

was making a mess of the water, the way a merganser gave up
on it altogether, settled on a rock to wait it out. Maybe
I'm waiting it out. Maybe saying hello

to my guardian angels—my mom, her mom, my Aunt Gloria—
is a good thing to do as I watch a piece of grass twirl.
Maybe, like Hạnh says, I need to adjust

to not having a lifespan, a self, a birth or death date. It's a lot
to accept: that we're *life without boundaries.*
The oak tree is the oak tree, he says,

but it's also the seed it was, though where's the freaking acorn?
That little nut is gone. It's like that part of ourselves
that will always be that kid doing cartwheels.

What's so great about going back into the void? As I shared with a friend,
we wouldn't be here without exploding stars,
so I guess it's best to focus on the clouds,

how fast or slow they're moving, the calamity
caused by wind, new leaves among
the dying fruit.

ACKNOWLEDGMENTS

Gracious thanks to the editors of the following magazines for publishing these poems, some in slightly different versions.

The Account: "Terminal Surreal" and "Abecedarian on a Friday Morning"
The Adroit Journal: "Can't Complain," and "There Are Thousands of Pleasures,"
Alaska Quarterly Review: "Abecedarian with ALS"
Allium: "The Busy Roadways of the Dead" and "Sometimes It's Nice to Be Taken Away"
Bennington Review: "I Have Thoughts Fed by the Sun,"
Couplet Poetry: "What I'll Miss" and "Orders of Operation"
Cream City Review: "A Poem about Twinflower" and "She's Pretty Much Who She Was"
diode poetry journal: "I didn't understand Keats's 'Ode to a Nightingale'"
The Glacier: "I am the last loss," and "It's Benzene, It's Ash, It's Lead,"
Hanging Loose: "Spas of the Mind" and "You-n-Me"
Image: "To-Do List"
The Indianapolis Review: "My Nineteen-Year-Old Daughter Is My Personal Assistant," and "How It Is Today"
Kestrel: "Flying Rats"
The Madrona Project, Empty Bowl Press: "Key Grove"
The Missouri Review: "When I Learn *Catastrophically*"
MORIA: "What's Terrible" and "John Muir Elementary"
ONE ART: "Self-Appraisal at 62" and "Postcard from Some Unknown Part of My Brain"

On the Seawall: "I Want to Be an Adirondack Chair"
Orion: "At the Mycological Society Survivors Banquet"
Pedestal: "Poetry,"
Poetry: "Is This My Last Ferry Trip?" and "Self-Elegies"
Poetry Northwest: "Mortal," "Smile," and "What I Didn't Realize"
Post Road: "Death Poem," "Elegy with Exhaust Fan and Robin Song at Dusk," "How to Fall," "If We Didn't Leave the Task to Backhoes," "Mistakes Were Made," and "When I'm on the Bed"
Presence: A Journal of Catholic Poetry: "When I Can't Get Out of Bed"
River Mouth Review: "Leo"
The Shore: "Possible Diagnosis" and "Why I Want to Be a Noble Gas"
Sixth Finch: "Unambiguously,"
Stone Circle Review: "Making the Best of It"
Tar River Poetry: "You Are Much More Than This Body"
THRUSH: "Since You're Alive" and "On a Bench Facing West"
Under a Warm Green Linden: "I Always Wake Up Happy"
Verse-Virtual: "I'm Not So Good at Corpse Pose"
Waxwing: "Before and After: A Quasi-Abecedarian"
West Trestle Review: "Poem on My Son's Twenty-Third Birthday"
Whale Road Review: "Why I'd Make a Great Chemist"
Willow Springs: "Portrait of Apple Cinnamon Mush, Chobani Yogurt Drink, and BiPAP"